THE JOURNEY
TO BETHLEHEM

THE JOURNEY
TO BETHLEHEM

Ronald B. Cox

iUniverse, Inc.
Bloomington

THE JOURNEY TO BETHLEHEM

iUniverse books may be ordered through booksellers or by contacting:

iUniverse
1663 Liberty Drive
Bloomington, IN 47403
www.iuniverse.com
1-800-Authors (1-800-288-4677)

ISBN: 978-1-4620-4191-6 (sc)
ISBN: 978-1-4620-4192-3 (ebk)

Printed in the United States of America

iUniverse rev. date: 9/15/2011

1 - A TRUTH STORY

Let me introduce myself. My name is Reuel and I'm not a writer. You might ask, "Then what are you doing writing this story?" That's a really good question. All I can say is that this story needs to be told and I'm going to tell it as best as I can remember.

If you're an astute reader, you might ask, "Did you make a mistake? When you said *truth* story, did you mean to say *true* story?" No! I want to be clear that this story is made-up.

In this story, it's not what the words say, it's what they mean. The words tell the story—the story tells the truth. It is important not only to see the story, but to listen to what is being said deep inside.

We live in a world of stories: books, magazines, newspapers, television, radio, and the Internet. And as so often happens when we read, or hear, or see a story, we are entertained. We are drawn into the story. We are happy when the characters are happy, and sad when they are sad. We are transported into the situation by the actions and words of the characters and the familiar and not-so-familiar locations.

I love stories and I would think you do as well. And not every story I've read is true. But of all the stories I have read, the really important ones cause me to think and wonder and dig beyond the words to find truth.

Now to be perfectly honest, this is not the best story that has ever been told. But I promise you this—the truth lies within the words.

Well, enough of that; it's time to get on with it. I'm not going to say, "Once upon a time," or "A long time ago," or "There was once," or even "In the Beginning." Let me just say,

"It's so sad."

2 - IT'S SO SAD

Talitha, Keturah, Kezia, Jael, and Rohgah were not only born on the same day, but their families lived next to each other at the end of a road out by the edge of the village. Because of this strange and wonderful circumstance, the families grew closer and closer, day by day, week by week, month by month, and year by year. They would help each other when help was needed and share when sharing made sense. Little by little, they became more than friends—they became a family.

You might ask, "Then why would you choose the title of the chapter to be 'It's so sad?'" Well . . . as the moms and dads grew closer and closer, over the years Talitha, Keturah, Kezia, Jael, and Rohgah moved in the opposite direction—they grew further and further apart.

They had been the best of friends. They had shared in sleepovers, birthdays, music lessons, synagogue, and so much more. They were inseparable—the fantastic five, five peas-in-a-pod, five fingers-on-a-hand, five toes-on-a-foot, five . . . well, you know what I mean.

But, as they grew, they changed—they grew away from each other. Their interests changed, their tastes changed, their friends changed, and it seemed as if their personalities changed as well. Instead of remembering those things that had brought them together, they only saw those things that were different.

"Why? You might ask."

3 - WHY? YOU MIGHT ASK

I don't know.

Talitha fell in love with art. She spent more and more time wandering the fields looking for colors and shapes—but missing the flowers, trees, and sky.

Keturah was a runner. She found a rhythm to her life in the movement of her feet and arms, but became isolated in the hours and hours on the trails.

Kezia wanted to be an innkeeper. She would haunt the local hostels until she persuaded an innkeeper into giving her a job. From that point on, every extra minute throughout the week was spent in learning the ins and outs of the business, but forgetting about the people.

And then there was Rohgah, the only boy in this group. As long as he could remember, it was the law that he was interested in. He wanted to make a difference and devoted himself to reading, studying, and learning. But, as with the others, he became lost in the books and isolated from his friends.

Jael was the musician of the group. She longed to hear new sounds and discover new poems. She spent hours upon hours perfecting her voice and training her ear. The time she spent with her music became time away from her friends.

Little by little they drifted away from each other, which sadly began to turn into animosity. "Why? You might ask." I certainly don't know. Maybe it was because they didn't share each other's interests. Maybe it was because they were too proud to be the first to say, "Hi! How ya doin'?" "Let's spend some time together," or maybe, "Are you ok?"

Whatever the reason, Talitha, Keturah, Kezia, Jael, and Rohgah slowly, but surely, lost their friendships—and some might say by default they gained an enemy.

The moms and dads were so busy with their lives that they totally missed any changes in their children. They recognized the accomplishments, but not the loss of friendships. They didn't notice the evolution from the 'fantastic five' to the 'fighting five' to the 'forgetful five.'

What happened?

4 - WHAT HAPPENED?

As the friendships of Talitha, Keturah, Kezia, Jael, and Rohgah fell apart, their lives moved in the same direction. They each followed their passion, married, had children of their own, and settled into a life filled with much; but not including each other.

Talitha became an artist. She explored the rural landscapes and captured the beauty of nature, the changing seasons, the fullness of spring and summer and the harshness of fall and winter. She had a circle of friends—but, not quite like her bosom buddies.

Keturah trained and became one of the finest runners in the district. She had many opportunities to be hailed as one of the best, but there was always the sadness of losing those who had been closest to her.

Kezia followed her dream and owned a local hostel. She had made a good living and had expanded the facility by opening a stable for the travelers' animals, and an eating establishment that achieved notoriety throughout the region as one of the finest places to eat. She met many, many people, but always felt sad that her best friends were not a part of her life.

Jael was the musician of the group. Her voice sounded like a bird singing. She would spend hours memorizing poems and perfecting her voice, but forgot that the most beautiful music was made by many voices, not just one.

Rohgah studied the law with the local Rabbi and traveled to learn from the best teachers. His studies took him to some of the largest towns and cities in the region and his reputation grew and grew and grew. He had returned several years ago and established a law practice in the village where he was born, which held so many fond memories, but the fondest were his long-lost friends.

They had just slipped away.

5 - THEY HAD JUST SLIPPED AWAY

How did it happen? How could five best friends end up as strangers? Strangers—enemies! Who's to blame? Anyone? No one? Everyone? How many times do we allow the most important things in our lives to slip away because we forget what's truly important, or, maybe, we just stop caring?

Were they tired of each other, bored, upset, angry, frustrated, jealous? It's been said, "Without a sense of caring, there can be no sense of community." Or maybe they lost the art of sharing. From their points of view, it wasn't their fault. Talitha blamed Keturah, who blamed Kezia, who blamed Jael, who blamed Rohgah, who blamed Talitha, who blamed Keturah . . . . Well, you know where this is going—nowhere! (It's important to know that the blaming of each other was never said out loud. It was only conjured up in their minds and felt within their hearts. Now that I think of it, it was probably the fault of each of them.)

As so often happens, the moms and dads missed a lot of the clues of this break-up and before they knew it, Talitha, Keturah, Kezia, Jael, and Rohgah were pretty much out of each other's lives and on their different paths. Every now and then they asked their children about their friends because it seemed that they hadn't seen them around lately. But it never went any further than an inquiry. Talitha, Keturah, Kezia, Jael, and Rohgah started down a road that would take them further and further from each other and seemingly in the 'blink of an eye,' they had grown up into careers, and families of their own, all without each other.

If our story would end at this point, as it sadly has in so many people's lives, this would be a tragedy. But, that's not the case.

Something happens.

6 - SOMETHING HAPPENS

Everyone was talking. In a far distant village, so the story goes, a child had been born. "Big deal," you say? Big deal, it was! For centuries there had been dozens of prophets and hundreds of prophecies proclaiming that a king would be born who would bring peace and justice and hope and possibility. You see, for these people, life was hard and harsh and difficult. Not that they were the unhappiest people in the world; however, in reality, life was tough. But, their religion promised that a king would come to make life better.

Because of the news, the synagogues were packed at every service as the Rabbi read and reread Psalm 22 and Isaiah 52:13 to 53:12. Following the services, the people would gather in the evening to search the skies for "The Promised Star."

This went on for several weeks until one night Namaah, the matriarchal elder of the village, called everyone out of their homes to look toward the eastern sky. And there, on the horizon, a star brighter than any other in the heavens shone with a beauty that could only be described as mystical, or magical, or incredible. Okay, there clearly was more than one word to describe "The Star." But, it was a light that filled the villagers with hope.

Now that in itself was fantastic. However, even more amazing was that, as the dawn broke, the star remained fixed on the horizon and was visible to even those whose sight was beginning to fail. Throughout the day, conversations filled with questions gave way to exclamations of joy and excitement. The normal activities of the day were peppered with smiles, laughter, and a growing level of heightened joy.

What could all this mean?

7 - WHAT COULD ALL THIS MEAN?

Namaah called for an assembly of all the villagers. She asked for them to meet her in the field by the fork in the river. The word traveled quickly and within the hour, the entire village filled the field. Namaah lifted her hands, motioning for the people to stop and listen. She recited from Psalm 22: "You who fear the LORD, praise Him! All you offspring of Jacob, glorify Him; stand in awe of Him, all you offspring of Israel! For He did not despise or abhor the affliction of the afflicted; He did not hide His face from me, but heard when I cried to Him. From You comes my praise in the great congregation; my vows I will pay before those who fear Him. The poor shall eat and be satisfied; those who seek Him shall praise the LORD. May your hearts live forever! All the ends of the earth shall remember and turn to the LORD; and all the families of the nations shall worship before Him. For dominion belongs to the LORD, and He rules over the nations."

She continued by reminding the people that as God's chosen, they were promised a Savior who would come to redeem his people and would rebuild the Temple. Namaah told those gathered that she had met with the Rabbi and astronomers. They agreed that the star in the East not only verified the birth of the King, but stood as a guiding light to the place of his birth.

She pointed to the eastern horizon and, in awe, the people stood in the silence of the evening. In the midst of their silence, the gentle sobs of joy-filled tears could be heard. As the sounds of weeping increased, voices of praise began calling upon the name of the Lord, with expressions of happiness that He had finally come back to save His people. Tears and cries of joy mingled as the people realized that this is what they had been waiting for—generation after generation.

This surely was the day of the Lord's coming.

8 - THIS SURELY WAS THE DAY
OF THE LORD'S COMING

Then the villagers stood and began clapping their hands, singing, and spontaneously dancing. This was a day like none other. This surely was the day of the Lord's coming. How exciting that it had happened during their lifetime. How blessed they were to be able to experience it.

In the midst of the celebration, Namaah asked the villagers to quiet down so that she could speak. It took a few minutes for the villagers to settle back on the ground. The air was rippling with joy and excitement.

As the villagers took their places, a small child approached Namaah. The child stood quietly, directly before Namaah with her head bowed. Namaah asked the child what she wanted—could she help her? Without a word, the child lifted her eyes to Namaah. Namaah noticed she had a small object in her hand. Namaah asked the little girl what she was holding. The child raised her hands and revealed a small handmade doll. Before Namaah could speak, the little girl said that she would like to give her doll to the newborn baby. She wanted to know if Namaah could take the doll to the baby.

With a tear in her eye, Namaah thanked the child, then turned to the crowd and told them that this child had offered her only possession as a gift for the newborn babe-king. She held the small handmade doll in her hands and lifted it for all to see. The entire village stood to their feet and cheered and cheered and cheered. Namaah motioned for the villagers to sit. But instead of calming themselves, shouts began to emerge calling for their village to send a gift to the newborn babe. Little by little the voices blended into a chant. Namaah again motioned that all sit—which they did.

Namaah gave the doll back to the child and thanked her. She proclaimed that in order to honor the newly born babe-king, they would bring greetings from their little village and offer a gift to honor his birth. The villagers cheered. She asked for volunteers, for it was a dangerous journey and those who volunteered would need to be willing to face those dangers.

The villagers looked from one to another. It was clear that their hearts were in the right place, but no one willingly stood and offered themselves for the journey. The villagers begged Namaah to choose the travelers and decide what gift would be best to offer a king. For she was the matriarch of their little village. Namaah agreed. She encouraged the people to return to their homes. She would spend the night in prayer considering what gift they should bring and who would be best suited to carry the gift to the newly born babe-king. Namaah slowly moved through the crowd.

She would seek the voice of God.

9 - SHE WOULD SEEK THE VOICE OF GOD

Namaah left the river and walked through the glade in the woods to the crest of the hill. It took her a little less than an hour to reach the crest. The path was an easy walk through the glade, but as she approached the hill she realized that what seemed like an easy climb during the day, was a little more treacherous in the night.

Upon reaching the summit, she fell to her knees, lifted her face to the heavens and prayed the words of Psalm 31:3: "You are indeed my rock and my fortress; for Your name's sake lead me and guide me."

She had accepted the responsibility to choose those persons who would journey to the babe. It had been many years ago that Namaah had been elevated as the leader of the village. She led the council of elders, arbitrated the quibbles and squabbles that so often crept into the daily lives of friends, neighbors, and families. She stood with the Rabbi at the births and deaths of the villagers and would often stand at the weddings, as well. She knew the villagers better than anyone else. They were not only neighbors—they were family.

In all of her years and in all the decisions she had made, this one would be the most difficult. Who would go? She knew that everyone had a willing heart . . . but she also knew that everyone had reasons not to go. She looked to the heavens and then to the Star. She wondered where the Star would lead. Would there be rivers to cross, mountains to scale, deserts to survive? She knew in her heart that it would have to be more than one person. She needed to choose a company of companions. A trip like this required strength, wisdom, endurance, and most importantly, loyalty to each other.

Who would she choose? Faces and names peppered her mind.

And . . . the gift?

10 - AND . . . THE GIFT?

Hers was a poor village. For as long as she could remember, the village had struggled to make ends meet. It's not that they weren't happy—for they were. It had been imprinted upon them from earlier generations that happiness was not dependent upon what they had, or defined by their abundance. Happiness was family, a home, hard work, and good health.

Life was hard, had been hard, and they expected it would always be hard. But paradoxically, life was good, had been good, and they expected it always would be good.

It's not that they didn't have years when the harvest was poor. They had—but they had just as many that had been good. It seemed, however, as if these last several years were challenging—extraordinarily challenging. The winters had been longer and harsher than memory could recall. And the growing seasons seemed to diminish ever so slightly year after year. The crops had been meager at best and the people were beginning to feel the harshness of life in a way they only remembered through stories told by the elders.

And . . . the gift? Namaah knew that the babe-king would be visited by all the leaders of the surrounding villages and by many from the great houses of neighboring countries. She could imagine gifts of great wealth and beauty that would be offered—treasures that were worthy of a king, but impossible for her little village to offer.

It would have been easy for Namaah to consider giving up. The task seemed beyond her ability to accomplish. In that moment of despair, she remembered that when a problem was beyond her capacity to solve, she must call upon the name of the Lord. The words of Micah fell upon her heart and mind, "Hear what the LORD says: Rise, plead your case before the mountains, and let the hills hear your voice." And that's exactly what she did.

She will wait upon the Lord.

11 - SHE WILL WAIT UPON THE LORD

The next morning the village was abuzz. Where was Namaah? Had she made her decision? Who would she choose to take the gift to the babe-king? And . . . the gift? Everyone had their questions—everyone had their opinions.

It was well after the noon-day sun when Namaah returned from the summit of the hill. She looked tired. As she entered the village, she stopped at the local hostel to freshen up and take some bread and drink. Within minutes the word traveled throughout the village. Everyone, from the youngest to oldest, gathered outside of the hostel waiting for Namaah to appear and announce her decisions.

What was only about twenty minutes or so seemed like hours. Little by little the villagers began feeling the excitement as the crowd gathered. Normally, the people would just sit and wait for any public statements. But not this day; no one was able to be still. The air was prickly with excitement.

Finally, Namaah appeared in front of the hostel. The people pushed in tightly around her to hear. They were so close it was impossible to tell one from another. They didn't want to miss a word. The owner, Kezia, carried a chair from inside the hostel for Namaah to sit. Namaah prepared to speak. She lifted her hands to still the crowd. They quieted. Namaah asked that everyone sit. The crowd, as one body, sat where they had stood. They intently strained to hear Namaah. What had she decided?

Namaah said that after spending the night and morning on the crest of the hill beyond the glade in prayer and meditation, it was revealed to her who should go. Without a whisper or sound, the villagers waited until they felt they would burst. Namaah paused. Finally she continued, saying that before she shared the names of those chosen to travel to the babe-king, everyone, without exception, must promise to abide by her decision.

Without hesitation, the villagers cheered and cheered and cheered. In one voice, they agreed.

Namaah stood and spoke.

12 - NAMAAH STOOD AND SPOKE

In her soft-spoken, yet impressively authoritative voice, Namaah announced that she had chosen five people to follow the Star. A gasp was heard from the villagers. It seemed as if everyone was attempting to guess whom she had chosen. And why were there to be five? Who were the travelers to be? Some said the rabbi, others, the local magistrate. Many agreed that the shepherds, who were so familiar with the land, were the perfect candidates for the trip.

Namaah raised her hand to quiet the crowd. She asked the villagers to let her continue. She said that there were to be five people in the band of travelers and she knew in her heart that they were the only five able to accomplish the task. She had chosen . . . Talitha . . . Keturah . . . Kezia . . . Jael . . . and Rohgah. You would have expected that after such a long wait to hear the traveler's names, that the villagers would have erupted in a joyful chorus. But no, that's not what happened. Upon hearing the names of Talitha, Keturah, Kezia, Jael, and Rohgah there was stunned silence. Without exception the villagers believed that these five, who were known so well, were the absolute wrong choice.

Slowly, murmuring grew into grumbling and slowly got out of control. Everyone was wondering why Namaah would have ever chosen *"those five?"*

Namaah raised her hand and quieted the people. She sharply warned them not to question her decision. As the villagers settled themselves, she called for Talitha, Keturah, Kezia, Jael, and Rohgah to meet her at her home at dusk.

The villagers dispersed in disbelief. The mood had turned from joy to shock. They were wondering what could have possessed Namaah to choose *"those five"* to undertake such an important mission.

Did she know what she was doing?

13 - DID SHE KNOW WHAT SHE WAS DOING?

With dusk approaching, Talitha, Keturah, Kezia, Jael, and Rohgah made their way separately to meet with Namaah. As each arrived outside of her house, they stood in silence. Clearly, the five were uncomfortable around each other. The wait for Namaah was becoming unbearable. In time, Namaah opened her door and invited the former 'Fantastic Five' to enter.

She asked them to sit. They moved cautiously, looking at Namaah and keeping a proper distance from each other. Opposite the fireplace there was a large bench that could accommodate four. Rohgah sat on one end while Jael sat on the other. They looked like bookends on a vast empty bookshelf. Neither Talitha, Keturah, or Kezia would sit between the two. "Uncomfortable with each other" could not even come close to describing the feeling that filled the room. It was much stronger than that. None of the five wanted to be close to each other. Keturah sat on a stool by the door, Kezia leaned on the fireplace mantle and Talitha stood awkwardly by the window.

Namaah settled in her chair and took some time to look fully in the eyes of each person. It could be said that she was looking into their souls. After several minutes of awkward silence, finally she spoke. She said that while waiting on the crest of the hill, she was visited in a dream. It was revealed to her that she would choose the five of them to follow the Star—to deliver the gift to the babe-king.

No one made a sound.

Namaah continued. She said that she could not force them to go. However, she believed in the very depths of her soul that they were the chosen ones. It was they, and they alone, who could make the journey successfully. Would they agree? Would they be willing to put aside whatever it was that separated them, to follow the Star and deliver the gifts to the babe-king?

Again, there was silence.

Who would be the first to speak?

14 - WHO WOULD BE THE FIRST TO SPEAK?

The silence was deep and dark. Namaah looked from face to face. One by one, the five avoided her glance by looking at the floor. Who would be the first to speak? Namaah said that whatever it was that drove them apart, it was now time to put it aside. She reminded them that there is a king who was born in the East. A king! The prophesied King! The "One!"

Jael was the first to speak. Looking at the floor she hesitantly said she would go, but . . . she would prefer to pick her own travel-mates! At that statement the other four snapped up their heads and drilled their eyes into Jael. Even though they were thinking the same thought, her remark made them look at her through eyes of anger and disgust.

Namaah replied that it was not for them to choose—it was for them to be obedient. Reluctantly, they agreed—each with a nod, grunt, or sigh. Rohgah asked when they were to leave and what gift they were to bring. Namaah replied that they were to leave in two days and it was their task to decide what gift should be offered from their village. Talitha, Keturah, Kezia, Jael, and Rohgah looked at each other, wondering why they should choose. Namaah sensed their quandary and told them that it was her wish and they were to comply. This was not a topic for discussion. She told them that it was her wish that they should meet, discuss the possible gift, and bring their suggestions back to her so preparations could be made.

Kezia loudly protested that it was hard enough to prepare for the journey without being responsible for picking a gift. Namaah would not be moved. She told them to return in two days. At that time she would give them final instructions. Namaah said that she would tell the Rabbi to expect the five of them tomorrow morning. They could use the synagogue in which to meet and discuss what gift to bring. Jael was about to respond, but Namaah stopped her and unceremoniously sent them on their way out of her house.

Off they went into the night.

15 - OFF THEY WENT INTO THE NIGHT

Not to each other, but in their minds, Talitha, Keturah, Kezia, Jael, and Rohgah were committed to meet early the next morning at the synagogue. Each would attempt to bring some ideas. They did not know how this was going to work. They had not spoken to each other in such a long time and tomorrow . . . it would be so odd and uncomfortable to be with each other, let alone speaking. But, they had agreed. They went to their homes to consider what gift should be offered to the babe-king.

Early the next morning, one by one Talitha, Keturah, Kezia, Jael, and Rohgah arrived at the synagogue. They entered and sat. Was anyone willing to speak first? Jael, wanting to get on with it, spoke up and asked if anyone had any ideas. In spite of being less than cordial with each other, Kezia was first to respond. She felt that they should take a collection from all of the villagers. Talitha disagreed. She retorted that they needed something that was more personal. (Besides all that Kezia was interested in was money, anyway!) Rohgah sarcastically responded that all Talitha wanted was to take one of her paintings. Talitha was indignant and demanded that Rohgah apologize. Rohgah then suggested a letter of welcome to be signed by all the villagers. Keturah chimed in saying how ridiculous the other four were. The villagers were poor, so there was no money to be had. Besides, most of the villagers could not even write, so a letter made no sense. Jael seemed to withdraw from the conversation—she just sat in the corner looking over her book of poems.

The disagreements and discouraging remarks continued until their anger became an impenetrable wall. Within minutes the discussion escalated to an argument and quickly evolved into moody silence. They sat, with backs to each other, fuming in their personal worlds of indignation.

The Rabbi, who had overheard much of the arguing, went to inform Namaah of the situation. She came immediately, entered the synagogue, and directed the five to follow her to the well in the center of the village.

The five adults, walking in a line like school children, followed Namaah to the well in silence with an occasional sigh or groan. Upon arriving, Namaah retrieved the bucket and cast it into the darkness of the well. She drew the bucket up and set it on the ground. It was full and spilling over. She asked each to cup their hands, take some of the water and wash their faces. Each of the five stepped forward and complied. She told them that washing their faces symbolized a new, fresh beginning. Now was the time to listen and stop the fighting.

This was their moment in time.

16 - THIS WAS THEIR MOMENT IN TIME

Namaah directed each to sit. As they sat, Namaah gathered the strength needed to complete her task of getting these five to accomplish what she knew had to be done. After inhaling a deep, long breath, she told them how disappointed she was in them. She knew that they had once been friends and that somehow that special connection had been lost. But this was the time that they needed to place the interests of the village above their own childish behavior.

Kezia motioned that she wanted to speak. Namaah dismissed her abruptly and told them all to keep silent. She had hoped they would work together, but she had her doubts that it would happen. During the night, she had decided what gifts would be taken to the babe-king. She told them that they either needed to agree to do what she directed them to do, or the journey would end right now. Decide! Now! And stop . . . wasting . . . my . . . time!

Embarrassed, Talitha, Keturah, Kezia, Jael, and Rohgah looked at each other and silently agreed with a nod that they would do as Namaah directed. Namaah thanked them and asked each to return home to prepare for the journey. The astronomers had calculated it should take no more than four days to complete. The five should be ready to leave at the setting of the sun tomorrow. Go . . . rest . . . prepare. Namaah said that she would meet them at the most eastern side of the village by the edge of the river.

As Talitha, Keturah, Kezia, Jael, and Rohgah left, they walked in silence with more questions than answers.

What would tomorrow bring?

17 - WHAT WOULD TOMORROW BRING?

Each of the five slept poorly. Oddly enough, however, as the sun divided the night from day, each awoke feeling refreshed. The day was filled with preparing for the journey and taking care of any loose ends at home. As the afternoon sun reached its zenith, Namaah dispatched a messenger to request that Talitha, Keturah, Kezia, Jael, and Rohgah come to her home prepared to begin their journey. They were surprised by the request. They had been told to be prepared by the setting of the sun. They didn't know why Namaah was calling for them early, but they responded and gathered everything together.

Upon arrival, each left their packs by the door. They entered Namaah's home. Each took the same positions as they had before. Namaah entered. Accompanying her were two of the elders. They carried a large wicker basket and placed it in the middle of the floor. The basket was of the finest quality. It was constructed in a tightly-woven, wishbone pattern. The top was connected to the basket with two beautiful gold and red chords. Attached to the sides of the basket were two long wooden poles. The elders placed the basket in the middle of the floor and left.

Namaah explained that she was convinced that the five would not be able to agree, so, she decided what would be the most appropriate gifts to send to the babe-king. She then reminded them, in a voice that was sharp and stern, that they had promised to deliver the gifts—without complaint and without hesitation.

She moved to the basket, unknotted the cords, lifted off the top and reached inside. One by one she removed the items from the basket and placed them on a table by the fire. There was a swatch of cloth, a length of rope, a jar of salve, a jug of water, and a pair of sandals. After placing the items on the table, Namaah settled back in her chair. She did not say a word—she sat in silence.

Namaah told each of the five to come forward and choose. Talitha stepped forward and chose the length of rope. Keturah was next and selected the jar of salve. Kezia and Jael took the jug of water and cloth respectively, leaving the sandals for Rohgah.

What could all this mean?

18 - WHAT COULD ALL THIS MEAN?

Talitha, Keturah, Kezia, Jael, and Rohgah stood in the middle of Namaah's room with the seemingly meaningless items in their hands, wondering what this all meant? A swatch of cloth, a length of rope, a jar of salve, a jug of water, and a pair of sandals! Was she serious? Were they really to undertake a dangerous journey to offer these . . . meaningless gifts . . . to . . . a . . . king? They were being asked to risk their lives to carry some insignificant items they could most likely purchase at any local market when they arrived?

Namaah sensed within her spirit their feelings of doubt. She reminded them that, due to their inability to work together, they had lost the opportunity to choose the gifts. Because of their disagreements and dissension, the choice had been left to her and now it was their responsibility to be on their way. They were to go to their homes . . . eat a meal and spend time with their families. She would pack and prepare the gifts for the journey. They were to meet at the eastern-most boundary of the village when the moon was at its zenith.

With looks of frustration, and a little bit of anger, Talitha, Keturah, Kezia, Jael, and Rohgah placed the items back on the table and walked to the door. Namaah spoke. They paused and turned to face her. She directed them to use their time wisely. There was much to do and little time. It was crucial that they reach the babe-king as soon as possible. She reiterated that they were to gather at the eastern-most boundary of the village when the moon had reached its zenith. Do not be late.

It was time for the five to be on their way.

19 - IT WAS TIME FOR THE FIVE TO BE ON THEIR WAY

The day moved from dusk into night. The moon, so round and bright, moved from the horizon until it almost stood overhead. One by one Talitha, Keturah, Kezia, Jael, and Rohgah arrived at the appointed place. Namaah, facing the East, was on her knees. She had made a small altar by placing five stones in a circle. Next to the altar was the basket holding the gifts. It was sealed with the gold and red chords and had the two long poles affixed to the sides for carrying. She requested that Talitha, Keturah, Kezia, Jael, and Rohgah kneel next to her. They approached in silence and slowly knelt.

Namaah lifted her hands toward the eastern sky—toward the Star. In her right hand were five seeds and in her left, five branches. As she lifted the seeds and branches to the sky, she bowed her head. She was speaking, but so softly that none of the five could make out what she was saying. After a moment or two, Namaah placed the branches on the altar and set a flame to them. As they began to smolder, Namaah stood and placed her hand on the head of each of the five. She said the branches represented the five of them. As the branches have been sacrificed to God, the five of them were sacrificing themselves for the babe-king. As she spoke, the smoldering branches burst into flame causing the darkness of the night to slightly recede. She then placed a seed in the mouth of each of the five, telling them to eat. This, she told them, was to represent new life and possibility.

Namaah continued by saying that as the light from the flame led the children of Israel to the Promised Land, the light of the Star would lead them to the Savior. She said that she wanted them to be like those branches. Namaah looked deeply into their eyes and spoke with the wisdom and authority of the ages, "Allow the spark of the Lord to ignite each of you so that the flame of God's Spirit will increase within you." She said she wanted the seed of life to grow in each of them as they journeyed. "Trust in each other and depend upon each other," she said. She told them that God would lead them . . . but the journey was theirs to make . . . the destination was theirs to achieve.

Namaah knelt by the altar and touched each stone. She looked up, touched the first stone and called out the name Talitha. Touching another she spoke the name of Keturah and continued speaking the names of Kezia, Jael, and Rohgah. She promised to keep this altar alive with fire until they returned. It will stand as a beacon to guide each of them home. Back home safe and sound.

Namaah stood, turned to face the five, and repeated the words of Laban, "May the Lord watch between you and me when we're unable to see each other."

"Now be on your way."

20 - NOW BE ON YOUR WAY

None of the five had ever been so far from their village. For each of them, this was the farthest they had ever traveled. Namaah had told them to follow the Star by the northern route. They would be traveling through the desert and then over a small mountain range.

The first day was hot and dry, but the traveling was fairly easy. The second day was much the same. But, by the third day, the five were beginning to feel the strain of the journey. The intense heat and dwindling water supply was beginning to take its toll. Little by little, they were becoming exhausted, and faster and faster frustration and anger were creeping upon their spirits. Their food and water were beginning to run out. Due to their weariness, thirst, and hunger, they were beginning to become careless. All that was on their minds was how to get this over with so they could be rid of each other and return home.

On the fourth day, the desert gave way to a rocky incline. It didn't seem too hard to manage. But, in reality, their weariness was taking its toll. After about an hour into their climb, they heard a loud scream. They turned to find Kezia, weeping, sitting on the ground. The four gathered around her and asked what had happened. She held up her sandal. She had made a mis-step, twisted her ankle, and fallen. What was she to do? Besides hurting her ankle, she would not be able to wear the sandal—it had snapped in half.

The other four came to her assistance. Rohgah helped her to her feet and walked her to a nearby boulder to sit upon. Keturah looked at Kezia's ankle and reported, happily, that the ankle was not broken, just badly bruised. The other three gathered around. They were pleased to see that the ankle was not broken. However, Jael noticed blood trickling from Kezia's forehead. Jael had never been very good around blood. That, coupled with the heat and her level of exhaustion, caused her to begin to swoon.

And she fainted.

21 - AND SHE FAINTED

In spite of her pain, Kezia shouted to the others to help Jael. They turned, and there before them, lay Jael crumpled on the ground. Talitha and Keturah ran to her. Keturah lifted Jael's head and placed it in her lap. She attempted to wake her, with no success. She called out to Rohgah to bring water. Rohgah looked in his backpack to discover that there was none. He called to Keturah and told her he had found none. She directed him to check all the traveling packs. He did, but with no success.

Rohgah called out that he was unable to find any water. Talitha told Rohgah to get the jug of water from the basket. Rohgah hesitated. Talitha commanded him to open the basket and bring the jug to her. He removed the cords, lifted open the top of the basket, and removed the jug of water. He carried it to Talitha. She asked him to remove the top. Again, he hesitated. She told him to hurry. He responded that this was a gift for the babe-king and it should not be used. Talitha sharply told Rohgah that the babe-king would not miss the water. This was more important. He opened the jug and poured the water into Talitha's hand. Because his hands were shaking, the water began to spill on to the ground.

Talitha told Rohgah to stop. She asked him to get the cloth from the basket, to tear a strip from it, soak it in the water, and bring it to her immediately. She was concerned that the heat of the day would be too much for Jael. Rohgah needed to act immediately. Reluctantly, but obediently, he did as she asked.

A strip of cloth was torn from the swatch, moistened, and brought to Talitha who applied it to Jael's forehead. She continued this for several minutes until, at last, Jael opened her eyes. Talitha told her to lie still.

Jael felt sick to her stomach.

22 - JAEL FELT SICK TO HER STOMACH

The heat was beginning to effect everyone. Fortunately, Jael was awake and beginning to recover. However there was still a concern for Kezia. Besides her ankle, when she fell she cut her forehead and it was beginning to bleed heavily. Keturah called to Rohgah to retrieve the jar of salve and bring more strips of cloth. Rohgah tore three or four additional strips of cloth and opened the jar of salve. He gave the items to Keturah, who cleaned the wound. In spite of the heavy bleeding, fortunately it was an extremely small cut. Keturah took salve and applied it liberally to the cut. She used the remaining strips of cloth to prepare a bandage, which she tightly fixed around Kezia's head.

With Jael recovering and Kezia's ankle and head attended to, the five sat, exhausted and emotionally drained. What were they to do? There was still a ridge looming ahead of them which needed to be reached before they could continue their journey.

In spite of the heat, they decided to start a fire. They would use the remaining water from the jug and combine all their food to prepare a hot meal. After a meal and some rest, Keturah felt that they would be able to complete their journey.

Rohgah gathered the wood while Talitha and Keturah prepared the meal. In spite of the simple ingredients, this meal was as tasty as any they had ever remembered. Following the meal, they decided that they would wait until morning to move on. Keturah felt that Kezia would be able to travel slowly, but travel she would.

As they settled in for the night, they began to share stories from their youth. Little by little, they began to open up and, unbeknownst to them, they were smiling, laughing, and enjoying each other's company.

Gently, they slipped into a deep and restful sleep filled with happy memories and pleasant dreams. Before they knew it, the night had passed.

Tomorrow arrived.

23 - TOMORROW ARRIVED

Jael was the first to awaken. It was hot and she was thirsty. As she sat up, the other four began to stir. Keturah checked on Kezia. A good night's sleep had done wonders for her. Her ankle was a bit swollen, but overall not too bad. Keturah changed the dressing on Kezia's forehead. The salve had done its job. The bleeding had stopped and what Keturah found was more of a lump than a cut. She helped Kezia to her feet and supported her. Keturah asked her to take a few steps. She hesitated, but did as asked. There was a little pain, but Kezia knew she would be able to continue.

Talitha called everyone to gather. They needed to start as soon as possible. There were still several hundred yards to the top of the ridge. She knew that they would have to depend on each other to make the summit. Talitha suggested that their first order of business should be to make sure that everyone was physically okay. Secondly, they needed to empty their packs and choose what they would take and what they would leave behind. They would also need to consolidate everything else. Rohgah brought up the basket with the remaining gifts. Jael asked what was left. Rohgah looked and reported that the only items left were the length of rope and a pair of sandals.

Spontaneously, they all began to laugh—except Rohgah. He looked puzzled and asked what was so funny. Talitha held up the broken sandal and pointed to the pair in his hand. It took a moment, then suddenly he realized what they were laughing at and heartily joined in.

Rohgah took the sandals from the basket and helped Kezia put them on her feet. They fit perfectly. Keturah, Jael, and Rohgah went about the business of emptying all of their packs. Together they decided what would be discarded and what would be carried. They also decided who would carry what and how they would proceed to the summit.

Keturah suggested that they abandon the basket, but take the rope with them. If this discussion had taken place only two days ago, the suggestion would have caused a fight and many hard feelings. Today, however, it was received with unanimous agreement.

They all agreed that Keturah should lead the way.

24 - THEY ALL AGREED THAT KETURAH SHOULD LEAD THE WAY

For the first time since they left on their journey, they knelt and recalled the reading from Exodus when Moses said to the Lord, "'If you really are pleased with us, show us your ways so that we can know you and so that you will continue to be pleased with us.' The Lord answered, 'My presence will go with you, and I will give you peace.' Then Moses said to him, 'If your presence is not going with us, don't make us leave this place.' The Lord answered Moses, 'I will do what you have asked, because I am pleased with you, and I know you by name.'"

Talitha asked the other four to find a rock. She wanted to build an altar like the one Namaah had assembled for them before they left. Talitha, Keturah, Kezia, Jael, and Rohgah each chose a rock. As they came back together, Talitha took the rocks and arranged them in a circle. She took the jug that had contained the water, held it above the circle and smashed it in the center. She said that as God had broken the walls of their indifference toward each other, so this jug is broken as a memorial to their faith and trust in Him. She lifted her hands toward heaven and prayed that the Lord God would direct their paths and lead them safely to their destination.

They looked to the summit and started on their way, with Keturah leading. She was followed by Kezia, Talitha, Jael, and Rohgah. Step by step, foot by foot, they moved toward the summit. They moved more slowly than Keturah would have wanted. As a runner, she had the greatest stamina. But she had become sensitive to the limitations of the others and moved at a pace that allowed everyone to feel comfortable.

After climbing for some time, it was clear that Kezia needed to rest. In spite of being close to the summit, Keturah stopped and suggested that everyone take a break. They had a little food, but no water. She encouraged everyone to eat something and rest.

As they did, she climbed to the summit. Upon reaching the top, she noticed that the Star that they had followed for so long, stood almost directly overhead. Walking closer to the edge of the summit, her eyes filled with tears as she realized that directly below her in the valley stood the village they had been seeking.

The end of their journey was in sight.

25 - THE END OF THEIR JOURNEY WAS IN SIGHT

Keturah wiped the tears from her eyes with the sleeve of her robe. She looked at the village, then back at the others, and offered a prayer of thanks. While standing at the edge of the summit, she looked for a way to descend. She noticed what seemed to be a path winding its way to the valley below. It looked passable, but treacherous.

She returned to the other four, who had recovered slightly from the arduous climb. Kezia was the first to notice how happy Keturah looked. She asked her "why?" Keturah told them that the village they had been seeking was in a valley on the other side of the mountain. With only a short climb left, they would be able to reach the summit and begin the descent to the village. And what excited her most was that there was a path! The four were more than happy with the news. In spite of being hungry, thirsty, tired, and bruised they were encouraged in their spirits. More than encouraged . . . joyful!

Talitha said they should start at once. They still had several hours left in the day and descending the mountain should be much easier than ascending. Keturah cautioned them that climbing down any kind of hill had its own inherent dangers. She wanted them to first focus on reaching the summit. Once there, they would prepare for the descent.

Rohgah stood and suggested that they be on their way. He turned to Kezia and asked if she was ready to move on? Kezia thanked him for his concern and told him if he would be willing to help her, she would be ready to go.

He offered his hand to Kezia.

26 - HE OFFERED HIS HAND TO KEZIA

Kezia grasped Rohgah's hand. Together they climbed toward the summit. Keturah led the way. Jael and Talitha followed behind. As the five moved up toward the summit, before them loomed the Star. Not only was the light guiding their way to the summit, it was also shedding light on the ground, allowing them to avoid tripping and the occasional pitfall.

The five were smiling, chatting, encouraging, and helping each other. Kezia thought she heard music. She did. Jael, spontaneously began singing. At first they couldn't make out what Jael was singing. Soon they recognized the words, "Baruch ata Adonai, Eloheynu melech haolam, shehecheyanu, v'kiymanu, v'higian u laz'man hazeh. (Praised are you, Lord our God, Sovereign of the universe, Who has blessed us with life, sustained us, and enabled us to reach this happy occasion in our lives.) The singing had a soothing effect on the five. They joined Jael. Some singing and some humming and Rohgah interjecting a strong and hearty whistle.

The Star, the smiles, the chatting, the helping each other, and now the music made them feel, in that deep and private place in their hearts and spirits, that this was going to be a great day.

The time passed quickly. They had lost all sense of their weariness. A few more steps, and the summit would be theirs. One by one, each stood at the very top. They felt as if they were on top of the world. They took in large gulps of air—cool and fresh and rich. They could feel energy returning to their arms and legs. They turned and looked at the vistas surrounding them. Behind them was the horizon from where they had come. In front, the horizon of the unknown. Above, the Star. Below, the village—the destination—the babe-king.

All that stood between them was . . .

27 - ALL THAT STOOD BETWEEN THEM WAS . . .

Keturah interrupted the moment. She reminded them that their destination lay below and they needed to be on their way. She suggested, that because the descent could be dangerous, they should use the rope to tie the group together. They agreed. Keturah tied the rope to her waist. She handed it to Rohgah—and one by one they snugly locked themselves to each other with the rope and prepared to move on.

Step by step, moment by moment, little by little, the band of five worked their way from the summit to the valley. They realized that they could not have accomplished the descent without each other. Were there moments of fear? Definitely! But, knowing that they were tied to each other gave them the strength to continue.

As they reached the valley, the sun began to set. Yet, the sky was alive with the light of the Star. It seemed to be pointing to the middle of the village. In spite of their hunger, thirst, and weariness, they had to find the babe-king. They just couldn't stop.

They removed the rope and walked toward the village. The closer they came, the more crowded the streets became. Soon they found themselves in a tightly packed crowd, shoulder to shoulder with little room to move. In spite of that, they pressed on. So as not to lose each other, they decided to hold tightly to each other by clasping their hands.

Little by little they worked their way to a small barn. And there, among the animals, was a feeding trough and a man and woman with a small baby nestled among the hay. Surrounding the family were many people. Some looked like shepherds; three of them were rather important looking dignitaries, and to their surprise . . ."Namaah!". The weary travelers called out her name. She turned, saw the five and rushed to them. They embraced. Keturah asked what she was doing here? Namaah replied that she had always planned on coming. She had decided she wanted to use this special event to bring the five of them back together. She knew that if she sent them by way of the northern route, they would either fail and return home, or work together and succeed. And here they were!

Jael confessed that because they had been so caught up in helping each other, they totally forgot about the past and became friends again. Talitha agreed, as did the others. Namaah looked at Kezia and said she was sorry she had been injured. Kezia replied that a small cut on her forehead and a twisted ankle was a small price to pay to have her friends back again.

Namaah invited them into the barn to see the babe-king. As they looked upon the child, Namaah told them to always remember how their coming to the Savior, Jesus Christ, had brought them back together.

Yes, back together.

28 - YES, BACK TOGETHER

For many years to come, Talitha, Keturah, Kezia, Jael, and Rohgah would gather each Christmas Eve to reminisce about their journey to Bethlehem. They had all come to realize the greatness of Naamah's wisdom and courage by choosing the five of them to represent their little village by bringing gifts to the newly born babe-king. They understood that the gifts that Naamah had chosen were not meant for Jesus. They were selected to help rekindle a love that Talitha, Keturah, Kezia, Jael, and Rohgah had shared and then had lost because of selfishness and jealousy.

Sadly, Naamah had died four years after that miraculous night in Bethlehem. Talitha, Keturah, Kezia, Jael, and Rohgah were glad that they had thanked Naamah for putting her trust in them. She may not be with them in body on those many Christmas Eves since her death, but she will always be alive and with them in the fullness of her memory and spirit.

Keturah giggled as she recalled the moment they first saw Namaah standing next to the manger that cradled that precious babe-king. How surprised they all were. The giggles were infectious and before anyone could help it, all five were laughing with such gusto, that tears began to roll down their cheeks.

In the midst of their tears of happiness, Jael began to express tears of sadness. The others stopped, embraced each other, and realized that the giving of one's self for others not only brings tears of joy, but of sadness as well.

Talitha, Keturah, Kezia, and Rohgah had come to learn that the greatest gift Naamah could give to the babe-king was the rebirth of love and friendship that the five had had, but had lost. And now, each of the five realized that the responsibility was theirs to give of themselves to others as Naamah had given of herself to them.

The evening passed quickly. Talitha, Keturah, Kezia, Jael, and Rohgah had plans and responsibilities of their own to the village and their families. As they gathered for that final moment together on the anniversary of the most important day of their lives, they were reminded that it all happened because they had traveled to see Jesus, the babe-king. They thanked God for Naamah. They thanked God for Jesus, the babe-king. They thanked God for each other. They thanked God for Christmas. They thanked God.

Pax,
Ron

Printed in the United States
By Bookmasters